Words for encouragement

A selection of devotional and inspirational poems

Some of these poems are based on life experiences

Written for words for encouragement.

dianechristian@hotmail.co.uk

Come home my child

Come home my child

For my Love for you I cannot hide

Come home my child

For to you my arms are open wide

I am sorry if somehow we have not been able to stay in touch

But you can be assured that I Love you very much

Come home my child

You are the apple of my eye

You mean everything to me

And that's the way it will always be

Come home my child

I'll welcome you no matter what you say or do

Come home my child

My Love will always be here for you

I understand if you need to take a little more time

For in my heart you'll always be mine

God always welcomes us back home with him he accepts us just as we are it's never too late to return to him. Like a parent who loves their child and welcomes them home God loves us the same he will never turn us away.

<u>Certainty</u>

Life is full of uncertainty

No one knows what is in store

But you can be certain that God will love you both now and forevermore

If you ever feel doubtful

If you're ever in despair

Just say a few simple words and he will hear your prayer

Try to be happy for the rest of your days knowing he will love you both now and always

Life can bring uncertainty but we can trust God to get us through every situation.

A breath of fresh Air

The Lord is like a breath of fresh air

You need him to stay alive

The Lord is like a breath of fresh air

You need him to survive

Every breath that you take is no mistake

God's love for you is real and is not fake

Even if you did not know the Lord in your youth

It's never too late to know the truth

He gave up everything for you and for me

He gave his life so we could be free

Gods' forgiveness to us he will always give

The Lord laid down his life so that we could live

God is a breath of fresh air to us he is for us and not against us.

The Lord is my shepherd

The Lord is my shepherd

He watches over me both day and night

He keeps me closely within his sight

The Lord is my shepherd

In him I am truly alive

He nurtures me and he makes me thrive

The Lord is my shepherd

He guides me down the paths that I should go

He strengthens me and he helps me to grow

The Lord is my shepherd

He stands by me through thick and thin

I know his voice and I always follow him

The Lord is my shepherd

I will always stay by his side

The Lord is my shepherd and in him

I will always abide

The Lord is the good shepherd who always looks after his sheep.

The loving father

The loving father guides us and strengthens us every single day

If we take a wrong path we hear his voice gently say

My child walk this way

 The loving father comforts us when we are in need

We know we are in safe hands when we always let him take the lead

He is the one who always understands

He keeps us close to his heart and holds us in his hands

The loving father is everything you imagine him to be

He is always willing to listen to you and to me

No matter if I am happy, sad or just feeling a little low

There is no other place that I'd rather go

If you're in a dilemma and not sure what to do

The loving father is the one who will help you get through

The loving father will turn your sorrow into laughter

He will make you dance with glee

God is the loving father and the loving father he always will be

Gods' love is unfailing he never gives up on us.

You are the light of the world

You are the light of the world

You are the light of my heart

From your love

I shall never depart

Nothing we have said

Nothing we have done

Can change your love

Your kingdom will come

No matter what people say

No matter what people do

Dear Lord we belong to you

The light of the world

The light of our heart

From your love

We shall never part

Jesus is the light of the world.

The spirit of the sovereign Lord is upon me

The spirit of the sovereign Lord is upon me I know and believe it is true

The spirit of the sovereign Lord is upon me it's plain to see in everything thing I have been through

His spirit is with me in my heart I feel that warm glow

His spirit is with me everywhere that I go

He is closer than a   sister or brother

There can never be another

The Lord will work through me as I come and go

For his Glory and for more people with him will come to know

He will shine his light in every smile

In every kind word

Stories of his love will be heard

The spirit of the sovereign Lord is upon me

But it's only by faith that I am free

Never will he leave you

Never will he forsake you.

Corners of the earth

Shout to the north the east the south and the west

Shout it out that Jesus is the best

May our voices travel afar

For God touches hearts no matter where you are

In the valley of dry bones far away

God made them flesh and was restored back to life that day

There is nothing he cannot do

To all the people from the corners of the earth

God can restore and heal you

Sing to the north the east the south and the west

Sing it out that Jesus is the best

Tell of his miracles and sing of his wonders too

There is nothing that he cannot do

He will hear you when you call

For Jesus is saviour to all. Amen

God given qualities

When Life tries to knock you down

Or things may look a little bleak

Hold on to God's promise that he choose you and appointed you and made you unique

He blesses you with individual qualities

That you can do

Because you are special to him and because he loves you

He uses you to bless others in your own way

Where your qualities are revealed each and every day

God has given special qualities to you

And he will continue to bless you in all that you do

Everyone has good qualities everyone has a purpose. Always know you have meaning in life to God.

A Sigh of relief

The Lord had given me a sigh of relief

Rescued me from pain and my suffering he did release

I am free from fear and As the Lords' peace starts to unfold

My hand he continues to hold

The Lord has helped me to stand

And the Lord has kept me strong

Keeping me in his Loving arms

Where I truly belong

I can't describe in words

The beauty of his great Love

And his Amazing Grace which he sends us from above

He is just always Loyal and true

The Lord rescued me

And the lord will rescue you

Jesus is our cornerstone he helps us stand firm and upholds us with his mighty right hand.

Because he cares

Because he cares you will sleep well tonight

Because he cares he will watch over you until the morning Light

Because he cares he will help you every single day

Because he cares he will shelter you from any storms of life that comes your way

Because he cares he will stay by your side forever and a day

Because he cares his love will never wither or fade away

Because he cares on lifes' Journey he will help you get through

Because he cares and especially because he loves you

God cares about the things that concern us he is interested in every part of our life and he will help us because he cares.

Your true worth

You are someone very special

And you have great worth

For God chose you and

Appointed you before your birth

From that first moment the seed he did sow

He protected you and watched you grow

He knows what things are on your mind

He knows the things in your heart

That you would like to do

For he gave those hearts desires to you

You are worth more than silver

You are more precious than gold

And in his hands you he will forever hold

He paid the highest price to set you free

From the power of sin

You are someone very special

And you will always be worth something to him

Everyone has a purpose in life and has great meaning we are worth something to God

His love is unconditional and he is there for us.

Unfailing Love

Gods' unfailing love is upon us

Morning noon and night

Gods' unfailing Love turns our darkness into light

His promises are alive

His unfailing Love nurtures us and helps us to thrive

His unfailing Love can always be found

His unfailing Love will always be around

His unfailing Love he poured upon me

His unfailing Love set me free

Nor height, nor depth, nor any other created thing shall be able to separate us from the Love of God   Amen

Power to change

God has the power to change

Us inside out

God has the power to heal

There is no doubt

God has the power

To help us overcome

God has the power

May his will be done

God has the power

To carry you through

Any situation

That concerns you

God has the power to change

Us inside out

God has the power to change

So let's sing in out

God can change any situation he makes impossible things possible.

Waves of forgiveness

The Lord offers us waves of forgiveness

Like gentle waves coming into shore

The waves of forgiveness are there for us all forever more

The waves of forgiveness gently cleanse our sins away

And refresh us everyday

No matter what we have done however big or small

The waves of forgiveness will wash away them all

To the waves of forgiveness we are all invited to go

Our sins may be red as crimson

But the waves of forgiveness will wash us whiter than snow

Jesus gave his life so we can be free

Through him we are right with God.

Jesus is coming back

Jesus is coming back

His return is very near

Jesus is coming back

But we have nothing to fear

He came once before

And our sins he bore

Jesus came for every one and for every nation

Jesus came for our salvation

Jesus is coming back

His return is very near

Jesus is coming back

For the ones he loves very dear

Jesus will come back for us for it is written Amen.

The horizon

On the Journey of life some

Times the horizon can seem so far away

But God helps us every single day

Every step we take is closer to tomorrow

An end to suffering an end to sorrow

Over the horizon is something new

Where many blessings are waiting for you

Life may still bring us trial

But the Lord stays by our side helping us through each situation giving us reasons to smile

Sometimes the horizon may look bleak

But God will Guide us and strengthen us when we are weak

The horizon is not so far away

With Jesus by our side helping us every step of the way

Sometimes things does not work out how we might hope but we know God has good plans for our future and plans for the good of us.

I will rise

I will rise when you call my name

I will rise if I am old or lame

I will rise with you on high

I will rise even if I die

When Jesus returns

I will see your face

I will rise up into your heavenly place

I will see you on your throne

My father in heaven the one who calls me his own

When Jesus returns

Everything will be as it should be

And we will be raised up with thee

When life gets us down God picks us back up

When we trust him he raises us up stronger than before

If God is for us nothing can be against us.

God blesses lives

God blesses lives

Sometimes out of the blue

God blesses lives including me and you

Sometimes Gods blessings are right in front of our eyes

Sometimes they come as a surprise

God blesses lives

I believe and know that it is true

So may God bless you

God blesses our life every day if we look we can see his blessings all round us.

Break every chain

Jesus has the power to break every chain

Giving us freedom and peace of mind of again

Nothing can hold us back

From nothing we have to hide

For Jesus is with us

He is on our side

The enemy tries to attack us

He is roaming all around we find

But we can stand firm

For the Lord gives us a spirit of Love strength

And a sound mind

Nothing can try to bind us again

For Jesus has the power to break every chain

God has the power to break any chain that tries to hold us back, no matter what has happened we have freedom through Jesus our Lord.

No greater Love

My life was full of doom and gloom

Until Gods' presence came and filled my room

His Unfailing Love touched my heart

His spirit touched my soul

A person who was once broken

Was now complete and was once again made whole

His Love is higher than any mountain

His devotion is deeper than any sea

His love is the most precious thing that was ever given to me

A Love so sincere so loyal and so true

Dear Lord there is no greater Love than the Love that comes from you

There is no greater Love than the Love of God for us.

Light at the end of the tunnel

There is light at the end of the tunnel

No matter how dark things may seem

There is light at the end of the tunnel

No matter how bad things have been

The horizon may look cloudy for some time

But after the rain God will make the sun shine

There is light at the end of the tunnel

So to your faith hold on tight

There sometimes may be a slight shadow of darkness

But God won't fail to show his Light

There is light at the end of the tunnel

Even when the enemy tries to make us whimper or groan

Hold on to God for in any storm of life with him you will never walk alone

God always shines his light no matter where we are he will be there for us

He makes the sun shine after the rain.

What a faithful God have I

What a faithful God have I

He smiles with me when I am happy

He comforts me when I cry

When I fall he helps me to stand

Always taking hold of my hand

Watching over me where ever I go

The greatest Love that I ever did know

He answers anyone when to him they call

What a faithful God have I and he is a faithful God to all

What a faithful God have I for he is always near

And he loves us all very dear

What a faithful God have I

He is faithful in all his ways

And he'll be faithful for the rest of our days

He is with us in all the things that we do

And never will he leave or forsake you

God is faithful and keeps all his promises.

If you believe

If you believe God will help you on your way

If you believe God will be there everyday

He will give you the strength to carry on

And fill your heart with joyful song

If you believe he will help you with everything

He will show you what to do

And pour out his love to you

If you believe there is nothing to fear

For God loves us and is always near

He keeps us close to him and he keeps us safe

And surround us with his grace

All things are possible if we believe faith as small as small as a seed can move mountains

God makes   the impossible possible.

You're the one

You're the one who opens our eyes

You're the one who answers our cries

You're the one that is always there

You're the one who will always care

You're the one who will catch us if we fall

You're the one who will help us with anything at all

You're the one with a listening ear

The one who takes away anything that we fear

You're the one who is with us in everything that we do

You're the one who lives in our heart and nothing can come before you

No matter what people do or say

Our Love for you is here to stay

You're the one that we adore

And we will follow you forevermore

Jesus is the only one who gave his life for us

The one who set us free the one that loves us no matter what.

I'm lost without you

Dear Lord

I'm lost without you

Is a line from a song

A line which says

You lost without us too

How you love to hear from us

You love to hear our prayer

When we feel lost we know you will be there

Like a father that misses his beloved child

You still love us in the times we may have once been wild

You guide our path

You set us straight

Your Love is eternal and it never comes late

So if we try to talk to you so much more

Then more abundance will be in store Amen

When we feel lost we know God is there like a loving father and he longs to hear from us just as much as we long for him.

Amazing God

I still stand amazed

How much God loves us

And turns dull days

Into bright sunny rays

How he showers us with love and is like water for our soul

How when we are broken he comes every time and makes us whole

No matter how many times life tries to trip us up and tried to make us drop

God is the one who always pulls us up back on top

I thank you Lord for your love so amazing and so divine

And i thank you Lord that you are mine

Thank you that you set us free

But most of all I thank you

That you came and rescued me

God is amazing his Grace and love are unfailing he never gives up on us.

No Barriers

There are no barriers to God's love

He gives us it freely from heaven above

No matter what things comes our way

He still loves us each and every day

He knows we will make mistakes

He knows we may not always get things right

But yet he is always with us

Watching us lovingly within his sight

There are no barriers to God's love

Your life he will truly bless

You can receive that love today

Just by saying yes

There are no barriers to Gods' love

He loves us unconditionally.

Faith

Faith is stepping out into the unknown

Faith is a gift from God in which we have grown

Faith is knowing all things are possible with God

As there is nothing that he cannot do

Faith as small as a mustard seed can have many prayers answered for you

Faith brings love peace joy and brings us healing

Faith is not been afraid to say how we really feeling

Faith gives us assurance of what we believe

Faith is a wonderful gift by Gods' grace that we can receive

Faith is something very special to me

It helps me do the things that before I never thought could be

Faith is a gift from God and all things are possible if we have faith.

Your goodness overwhelms me

You're goodness overwhelms me

I can scarily take it in

You broke my chains and freed me from sin

You showed me love and compassion

And pulled me out the deep dark pit

And in my life your light you lit

You made my darkens bright

And stood by me both day and night

You still loved me when I did things that I wanted to do

And now my life I give back to you

I am sorry for the times I may have had doubt

And my life with you I cannot be without

God is good even in times where we feel not at our best

He carries us through our storms of life and keeps us strong.

You never let go

When people come into our life

And shatter our hopes and dreams

It feels like we on an emotional roller coaster ride

But the Lord Will away stay by our side

He will hold on to us and help us to stand firm

As we grow and as we learn

When we are hurting he will comfort us and help us every step of the way

And he will keep on Loving and blessing us every single day

He will wrap his arms around us in a warm embrace

And he will constantly watch over us in each and every place Amen

With God's help we will do mighty things

For he will trample down our foes.

My Anchor

The Lord is my anchor in the storms of life

The Lord is my anchor

Who carries my cares and strife

The Lord is my anchor to whom

I hold on tight

The Lord is my anchor

Who makes everything all right

The Lord is my anchor

He catches me when I fall

The Lord is my anchor

My one and my all

As an anchor for the soul firm and secure. Like an anchor holding a ship safely in position

Our hope in Christ guarantees our safety.

Prayer

Even in the times I'm not sure what to say when I pray

God still hears every word that I need to say

Sometimes he likes us just to be still and to listen to him

Open our hearts and let him in

He knows all the things that we need and the things that are in our heart

So when it comes to praying he will always help us where to start

No matter if we sitting, standing, laying, kneeling, sleeping, or cooking the tea

He always listens to you and to me

Just focus on him the rest will fall into place he will always show us where to begin

Just open your heart and let him in

He hears our every word he listens to our heart

And from our side he will never part

So if we speak out loud or just need to have a quiet prayer

God will hear us and God will always be there. Amen

Therefore I tell you, whatever you ask for in prayer, believe that you have received it, and it will be yours. Amen.

A Fresh start

Yesterday has been and gone

Today is a new day to start from

Whatever our background

No matter where we have been

God loves us he wipes our slate clean

He will stand by us both day and night

He is compassionate and graceful

He called us by our name and we belong to him

Jesus wipes our slate clean giving us a fresh start every single day. We have the chance to start afresh if things have not been so good.

It's never too late

It's never too late to say sorry

It's never too late to say that you care

If someone needs your help

It's not too late to say that you'll be there

It's never too late to change your life

Or too change the path that you go

It's never too late to share good news with someone that you know

Gods' Love is for everyone his love his here to stay

It's never too late to come back to him today.

Yesterday today and tomorrow his love remains the same

We have nothing too loose but we have everything to gain

We don't have anything to fear or too hide

He welcomes us all with his arms open wide, it's never too late

He is always there for us.

Acceptance

There are parts of our life which we might regret

But with God in your life he helps you forget

Weather we are near or far

He loves us for who we are

We are precious to him

He frees us from all our sin

And if you believe in him then a new life for you can begin

With God we have nothing to hide

For he welcomes us with his arms open wide

He will turn your life around

Just give yourself back to him today

For he loves you and will never turn you away

God accepts us just as we are he loves us with an everlasting love.

Fountain of life

As our journey with Jesus does begin

Our hearts are like a fountain that bubbles up

And overflows from the spirit within

Like a river it flows and flows

Strengthening us and our faith grows

Refreshed and all things are made new

When the spirit of the Lord falls upon you.   Amen

The Lord will guide you always; he will satisfy your needs in a sun-scorched land and will strengthen your frame. You will be like a well-watered garden, like a spring whose waters never fail.

I Am

I Am the Way the Truth the Life

I Am the Bread of Life and I Am the True Vine

I Am the One who called you by name and you are mine

I Am the One who sets you free

I Am the One who went to Calvary

I Am the Alpha the Omega the Beginning and the End

I Am the One who calls you friend

I Am the one who created man

I Am Who I Am

He is the Great I Am Who Is and was and is to come Amen.

God is great

God is great God is strong

Watching over us with love keeping us safe in the shadow of his wings where we belong

The Lord gives and the Lord takes away

But no matter how sad things are I will thank the Lord every single day

Some people come into our life and some people go

But God never leaves us this I do know

So no matter how much life tries to make you give in

Stay close to Jesus for with him the battle he always will win

he goes before us to guide our way, he stands behind us to catch us if we fall and stand beside us in everything that we do, nothing can ever separate us from the Love of God, we grow in his love every day and we sing his praises regardless of how much life hurts us, just keep singing and praying and standing with God, first in our hearts king forever. Prince of peace Amen

We will be restored

When our lives come crashing down

Around us like a hurricane

The Lord will build us back up

And restore us once again

And as he picks us up piece by piece

All our hurt and pain he will release

He will melt us and mould us

And make us even stronger than before

And our broken lives he will restore.

God will restore the years the locusts have eaten away   Amen

The rainbow

When I see a rainbow

 Red, orange, yellow, green and blue

Reminds me Lord of the beauty of you

I think of a pot of gold

Which are your words which were for told

I think of golden coins and how you treasure each and every one

You count us very closely and never miss out anyone

Every time a rainbow has rose

Reminds me that we are the ones that you have chose

Your Love comes in great lengths it's impossible to measure

We are your little golden coins that you sincerely treasure

So when I see a rainbow

Red, orange, yellow, green and blue

Reminds me of just how much we mean to you.

No mere man has ever seen, heard or even imagined what wonderful things God has ready

For those who Love the Lord. Amen

God's beautiful creation

God's creation is beautiful

From the scenery right down to the birds that sing

God's creation is beautiful in each and everything

God's creation is beautiful if we look around we will see

God's creation is beautiful

Including you and me,

When you look up at the stars at night, always remember that you are precious in his sight,   wow God bless you all

How majestic his Name Amen.

Lifted Up

The Lord lifts us up when things get rough

The Lord lifts us up when times get tough

The Lord lifts us up when we are down

And feel we have been trodden upon

The Lord lifts us up the one we can truly always rely on

The Lord lifts us up whatever is thrown our way

The Lord lifts us up each and every day

The Lord lifts us up we just have to give him a call

The Lord lifts us up from any situation at all.

Thank you Lord for your promises of restoration.

the meadow

In the meadow the pastures are green

With a gentle running stream

Into the meadow we can go

Where lots of lovely flowers grow

In the meadow the Lord is there

With lots of lovely things to share

In the meadow we are free

Where we can live life abundantly Amen.

<u>Timing</u>

When there is something on our hearts

And we are waiting for things to come

 Sometimes it can feel like a long time

But God's will be done

God's Timing is perfect

It is never too early or too late

The Lord brings all good things

And renew the strength of those that wait

God does things at the right time

At the right place

Bringing joy to our hearts and a smile to our face Amen

 God promises that these things I plan won't happen right away. Slowly, steadily, surely, the time approaches when the vision will be fulfilled. If it seems slow, wait patiently, for it will surely take place. It will not be delayed. Amen

Seeds

Plant a seed and watch it grow

Plant a few more in a row

There you see God's love grow

When you see them bloom

And the beauty in that you do

This is how God sees you

God sees the true beauty in everyones heart,

When we share his love with others we plant seeds for god

And he watches them grow into his beauty and likeness

His life living water makes us grow and nurtures us. Thank you God

That you make us into the people you want us to be Amen,

A poem my son wrote and wanted to share in this book.

Love is

Love is a happy place to show your love to Jesus and God

Love is a treasure it a gift from God

God's love is for all to share so tell people everywhere about God love.

God is love

Jesus is love

The Holy Spirit is love

Reading God word is lovely

For he is the only one that I can trust

So forget about all the rest

For he the one who always knows best

Trust no one but God, love Leanne

A poem my daughter wrote and wanted to share in this book.

Choices

The choices we make in life

Can be good ones or bad

But there is one choice I made

That I will be forever glad

The day I gave my life to the Lord

And stopped doing things on my own accord

I gained so much confidence

That will never fade

Regardless of everyone making me feel

Like I'd never make the grade

People used to say I cannot write

They said I could not sing

But that important choice I made

Changed everything

I am a published poet

And have wrote new songs to sing

Giving my life to Jesus taught me

Through him I can do anything

The choice to follow him

Is the day I will never forget

The best choice in life that   I will never regret.   Amen

Printed in Great Britain
by Amazon